24 HOUR HISTORY

THE APOLLO 11 MOON LANDING

JULY 20, 1969

Nel Yomtov

Heinemann
LIBRARY
Chicago, Illinois

To contact Capstone Global Library please phone 800-
747-4992, or visit our Web site www.capstonepub.com

Edited by Adam Miller, Abby Colich, and
    John-Paul Wilkins
Designed by Steve Mead
Original illustrations © Advocate Art 2014
Illustrated by Andrew Chiu
Production by Victoria Fitzgerald
Originated by Capstone Global Library Ltd

Library of Congress Cataloging-in-Publication Data
Nel Yomtov
The Apollo 11 moon landing : July 20, 1969 / Nel
Yomtov.
      pages cm.—(24-Hour History)
   Includes bibliographical references and index.
   ISBN 978-1-4329-9292-7 (hb)—ISBN 978-1-4329-9298-
9 (pb)

   2013935059

Acknowledgments
We would like to thank Geza Gyuk for his invaluable
help in the preparation of this book.

Printed in the United States of America in
North Mankato, MN. 092015 009197RP

CONTENTS

Countdown to a Moon Shot...................... 4

Destination: Moon!............................... 6

"The *Eagle* Has Landed"........................14

"One Giant Leap for Mankind" 24

The Legacy of *Apollo 11* 38

Timeline.. 40

Map of Command Module Splashdown 41

Cast of Characters 42

Glossary 44

Find Out More 46

Index 48

Direct quotations are indicated by a yellow background.

Direct quotations appear on the following pages: 5, 8, 12, 13, 17, 22, 23, 25, 28, 29, 30, 31, 32, 33, 37.

In 1956, the United States and the Soviet Union both announced plans to launch an Earth-orbiting satellite the following year. On October 4, 1957, the Soviets launched the satellite, *Sputnik*.

In January 1958, the Americans sent the *Explorer 1* satellite into low Earth orbit. The Space Race was on.

The Soviets sent the first human into space—Yuri Gagarin—in April 1961.

Meanwhile, the Americans were hard at work on their own space program.

On May 5, 1961, astronaut Alan Shepard became the first American to travel into space.

Three weeks later, U.S. president John F. Kennedy made an important announcement to Congress.

I believe this nation should commit itself to achieving the goal, before this decade is out, of landing a man on the Moon and returning him safely to the Earth.

Over the following eight years, NASA conducted a series of missions to prepare for a manned moon landing.

Finally, on July 16, 1969, at 9:32 a.m. local time (EDT), *Apollo 11* was launched from the Kennedy Space Center in Florida. Aboard the spacecraft were astronauts Neil Armstrong, Michael Collins, and Edwin "Buzz" Aldrin. Their target: Earth's moon—238,900 miles (384,400 kilometers) away.

6:20 A.M.

Three hours earlier, the astronauts had left the Manned Spacecraft Operations Building at the Kennedy Space Center. They boarded a van for a short ride to the launch pad.

You boys have a safe flight.

We will. You take yourself on a nice vacation, Joe.

Suit technician Joe Schmitt rode with the astronauts, making last-minute checks on their suits.

More than one million eager onlookers gathered on the nearby roads and beaches to watch the historic launch. A worldwide audience of around one billion people followed the action on television.

GOODLUCK!

GOOD LUCK APOLLO

APOLLO 11

THE MAN BEHIND THE MISSION

Wernher von Braun (1912–1977) was a German-American rocket scientist who developed the *Saturn V* rocket that launched the Apollo missions into space. During World War II (1939–1945), von Braun developed combat rockets for the Nazi regime. In May 1945, he surrendered to American officials. Rather than face trial for aiding the enemy, von Braun agreed to work for the U.S. government. He was brought to the United States to work on its space program. Von Braun and members of his German rocket team also helped pioneer the development of the two-vehicle Command Module and Lunar Module systems. In 1975, he was awarded the National Medal of Science by the U.S. government.

Former president Lyndon B. Johnson and then vice president Spiro Agnew proudly watched the launch from the viewing stand. They were among the thousands of specially invited guests that included congresspeople, governors, NASA officials, and foreign ministers.

There it goes!

We did it! Go! Go!

FAST FACT

The Kennedy Space Center is located on Merritt Island, Florida, west of Cape Canaveral on the Atlantic Ocean. It is 34 miles (55 kilometers) long and about 6 miles (10 kilometers) wide, and covers an area of about 220 square miles (570 square kilometers). It has been the launch site for every NASA human spaceflight since 1968.

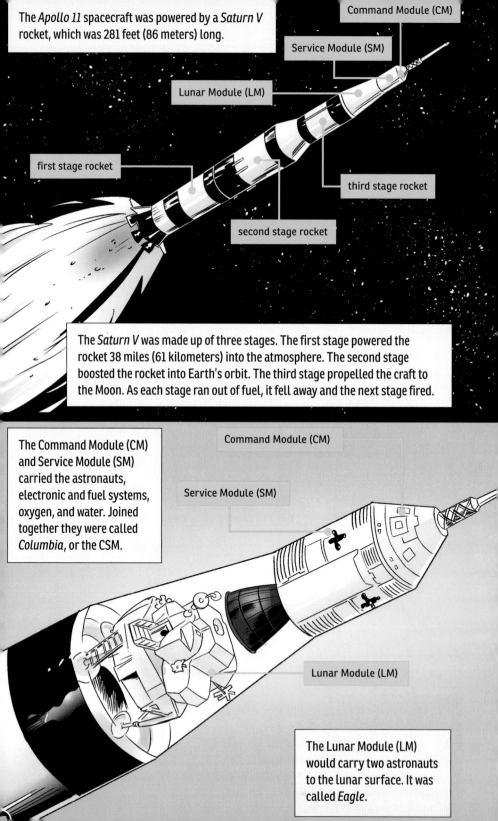

The *Apollo 11* spacecraft was powered by a *Saturn V* rocket, which was 281 feet (86 meters) long.

Command Module (CM)

Service Module (SM)

Lunar Module (LM)

first stage rocket

third stage rocket

second stage rocket

The *Saturn V* was made up of three stages. The first stage powered the rocket 38 miles (61 kilometers) into the atmosphere. The second stage boosted the rocket into Earth's orbit. The third stage propelled the craft to the Moon. As each stage ran out of fuel, it fell away and the next stage fired.

The Command Module (CM) and Service Module (SM) carried the astronauts, electronic and fuel systems, oxygen, and water. Joined together they were called *Columbia*, or the CSM.

Command Module (CM)

Service Module (SM)

Lunar Module (LM)

The Lunar Module (LM) would carry two astronauts to the lunar surface. It was called *Eagle*.

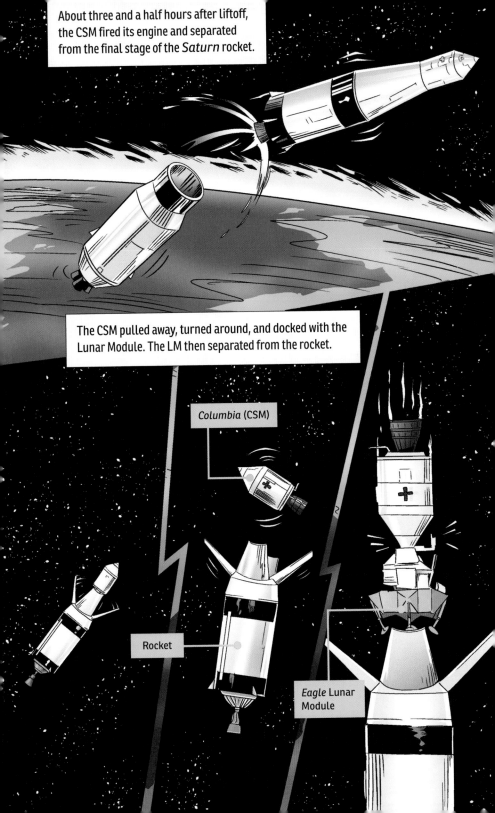

About three and a half hours after liftoff, the CSM fired its engine and separated from the final stage of the *Saturn* rocket.

The CSM pulled away, turned around, and docked with the Lunar Module. The LM then separated from the rocket.

Columbia (CSM)

Rocket

Eagle Lunar Module

What's for Dinner?

The crew of *Apollo 11* had more than 70 choices of food on their menu. Many of the items were freeze-dried and could be eaten after adding water. Others were kept wet in plastic packs. Among the selection were beef and potatoes, tuna salad, and hot dogs. Beverages included orange drink, grape punch, and cocoa. The dessert menu included fruitcake, banana pudding, and brownies.

SEA OF TRANQUILLITY

The site where *Apollo 11* landed is called the Sea of Tranquillity. This is translated from its Latin name *Mare Tranquillitatis*. Italian astronomers Francesco Grimaldi and Giovanni Riccioli named the site in 1651. The Sea of Tranquillity is not a sea of water. In fact, it is a large, dark, rocky plain that was formed by volcanic eruptions. The area has a bluish color due to the metal in the soil and in the rocks, which are made of basalt.

For the next seven hours, the astronauts ran through the long checklist of equipment they needed to venture out onto the lunar surface. When they were finished, they helped each other into their bulky space suits.

Armstrong opened a hatch that exposed a television camera. The camera would show people around the world the historic moonwalk.

Meanwhile, *Columbia* orbited on the other side of the Moon. Out of communication range, Collins would be unable to hear Armstrong as he stepped onto the lunar surface.

In his space suit, Armstrong prepared to exit *Eagle*.

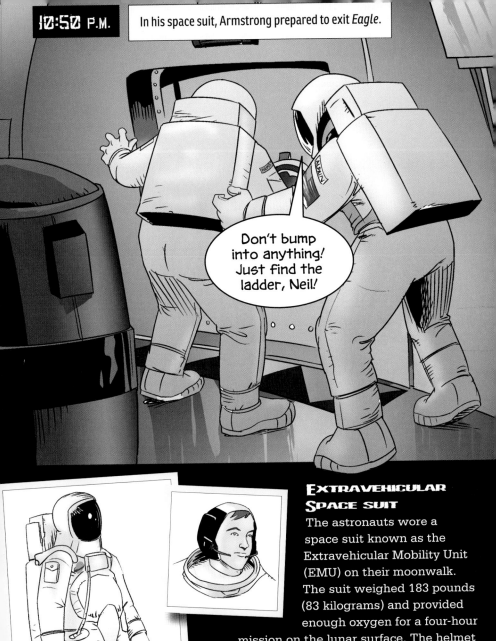

Don't bump into anything! Just find the ladder, Neil!

Extravehicular Space Suit

The astronauts wore a space suit known as the Extravehicular Mobility Unit (EMU) on their moonwalk. The suit weighed 183 pounds (83 kilograms) and provided enough oxygen for a four-hour mission on the lunar surface. The helmet was equipped with two visors that offered temperature control and protection against small meteors and dangerous ultraviolet light. Communication between the astronauts and Mission Control was made possible by "Snoopy hats." These devices fit over the astronauts' head and ears, and contained microphones and earphones. They were worn under the helmet.

FAST FACT

Armstrong's "one small step" wasn't actually that small. He had landed *Eagle* so gently that its shock absorbers didn't fully close. He had to hop 3.5 feet (1.1 meters) from the *Eagle*'s ladder to the surface!

On July 20, 1969, Neil Armstrong became the first human to set foot on the Moon.

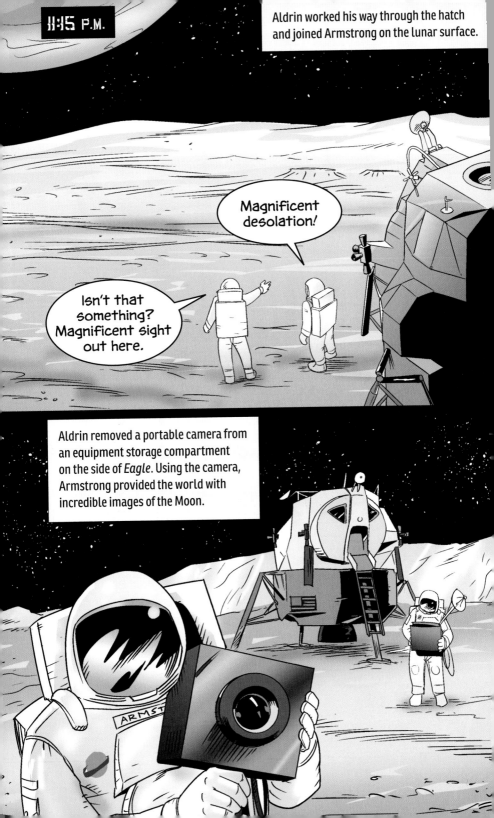

Aldrin's next assignment was to test the Moon's gravity. On the lunar surface, he weighed only one-sixth of his weight on Earth. Aldrin joyfully became the first human to do the "kangaroo hop"!

Watching TV back on Earth, Aldrin's wife, Jean, laughed so hard that she cried.

The astronauts then received an important phone call from President Nixon.

11:48 P.M.

Hello, Neil and Buzz, I'm talking to you by telephone from the Oval Room at the White House....For every American, this has to be the proudest day of our lives....Thank you very much.

FAST FACT

President Nixon had a speech ready in case the astronauts missed being picked up by the orbiting Command Module. It read, "These brave men, Neil Armstrong and Edwin Aldrin, know that there is no hope for their recovery. But they also know that there is hope for mankind in their sacrifice."

As Armstrong returned to collecting a large sample of lunar rocks...

Watch it, Neil! You're on the TV cable!

Whoa! I can't see my feet very well with this helmet visor, and my boots are so thick I can't feel that I'm on the cable!

Aldrin took a photo of the imprint his boot made in the lunar surface. It has become one of the most famous photos in history. Then he snapped shots of *Eagle* to show NASA engineers the condition of the craft.

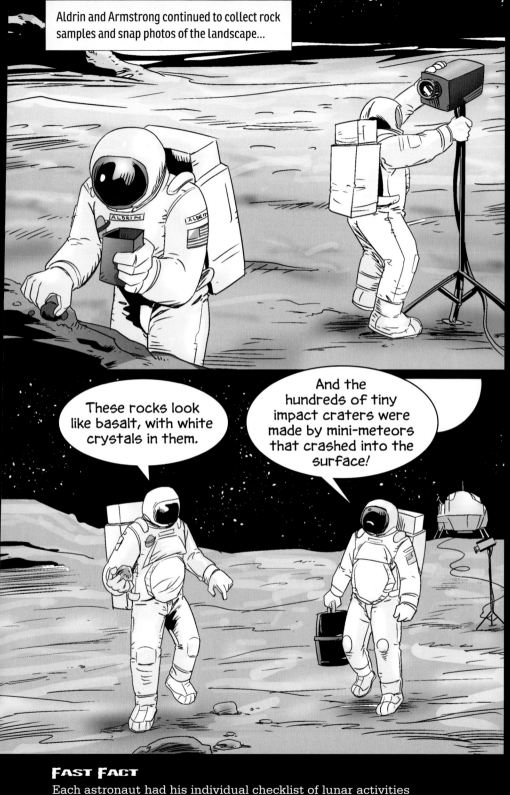

THE LEGACY OF APOLLO 11

After reentering *Eagle*, Armstrong and Aldrin remained on the Moon's surface in the LM for ten more hours. Finally, on July 21 at 1:54 p.m., *Eagle* blasted off from the lunar surface to begin redocking operations with Collins, who was still orbiting the Moon in *Columbia*. At 12:50 p.m. on July 24, the Command Module, the only part of the spacecraft to return through Earth's atmosphere, splashed down in the Pacific Ocean. The spacecraft—carrying three tired but cheerful and grateful astronauts—was recovered by the aircraft carrier USS *Hornet* minutes later.

Armstrong walked on the Moon for a total of 2 hours, 37 minutes and 37 seconds, and Aldrin for around 40 minutes less. Yet the legacy of *Apollo 11*'s crew—Armstrong, Aldrin, and Collins—will be felt for many generations to come. By making President Kennedy's dream a reality, the world viewed the United States as a more scientifically advanced nation than its rival, the Soviet Union. The successful landing also established American technological and engineering dominance over all other countries.

The Apollo missions rapidly sped up the pace of technology development, especially in the United States. The technology used to put Americans into space was used to develop computer hardware and software, robotics, national defense, transportation, food processing, and improvements in health care. Thousands of everyday products also come from space program technology, including fabrics for clothing and shoes, cordless power tools, and lighting systems. The Internet also owes a huge thanks to the space program.

Apollo 11's success encouraged many nations to begin their own space programs. Since 1969, France, Korea, Poland, Iran, China, Bulgaria, and many other countries have founded their own space agencies. The International Space Station (ISS), the most complex international scientific project in history, is another example of *Apollo 11*'s far-reaching legacy.

Many people around the world still consider *Apollo 11* the greatest achievement of the 20th century. We will always remember that moment not only for humans setting foot on the Moon, but also for leaving planet Earth in search of a new and promising future.

TIMELINE

October 4, 1957	Soviets launch *Sputnik* satellite
November 3, 1957	Laika, a Russian dog on board *Sputnik 2*, becomes the first animal to orbit Earth
April 12, 1961	Soviets send a human into space for the first time
May 5, 1961	Alan Shepard becomes the first American to travel into space
May 25, 1961	President John F. Kennedy urges the United States to land a man on the Moon "before this decade is out"
1961–1969	United States conducts numerous space projects, including the Mercury, Gemini, and Apollo missions
November 22, 1963	President Kennedy is assassinated in Dallas, Texas
July 16, 1969, 9:32 a.m.	*Apollo 11* launches from Kennedy Space Center in Florida
July 20, 10:02 a.m.	Aldrin and Armstrong move from *Columbia* Command Module to *Eagle* Lunar Module to prepare for undocking
12:44 p.m.	*Columbia* and *Eagle* complete successful undocking
2:08 p.m.	*Eagle* prepares for powered descent
3:17 p.m.	*Eagle* lands on lunar surface
10:50 p.m.	Armstrong prepares to exit *Eagle*
10:56 p.m.	Armstrong becomes first human to step on the Moon
11:09 p.m.	Armstrong collects contingency samples
11:15 p.m.	Aldrin joins Armstrong on lunar surface
11:41 p.m.	Astronauts plant American flag on Moon surface
11:48 p.m.	President Richard Nixon speaks to Armstrong and Aldrin
July 21, 1:11 a.m.	Hatch to *Eagle* is shut; moonwalk officially ends
1:54 p.m.	*Eagle* blasts off from lunar surface
July 24, 12:50 p.m.	Command Module carrying Armstrong, Aldrin, and Collins splashes down in the Pacific Ocean

MAP OF COMMAND MODULE SPLASHDOWN

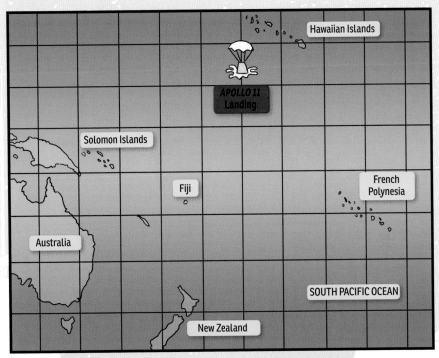

Hawaiian Islands

APOLLO 11
Landing

Solomon Islands

Fiji

French
Polynesia

Australia

SOUTH PACIFIC OCEAN

New Zealand

CAST OF CHARACTERS

Lyndon B. Johnson (1908–1973)
Johnson was the 36th president of the United States. LBJ, as he was commonly known, took office upon John F. Kennedy's assassination in 1963. Johnson believed a successful moon launch would be a great contribution to America's image around the world. Much of Apollo's research and development came during his time in office, from 1963 to 1969.

Richard M. Nixon (1913–1994)
Nixon was the 37th president of the United States and held office at the time of the *Apollo 11* moon landing. He believed the U.S. space program was important for exploration, to gain scientific knowledge, and to apply the lessons learned in space to benefit people on Earth. He watched the moon landing from his office and spoke to Armstrong and Aldrin shortly after they stepped onto the lunar surface. Nixon called his conversation with the astronauts "the most historic telephone call ever made from the White House."

John F. Kennedy (1917–1963)
Kennedy was the 35th president of the United States. He was determined that the United States should defeat the Soviet Union in the Space Race. In May 1961, he urged Congress to support the goal of landing a man on the Moon and returning him safely to Earth within the decade of the 1960s. He was assassinated in Dallas, Texas, on November 22, 1963, less than three years into his term in office.

Edwin "Buzz" Aldrin Jr. (b. 1930)
Aldrin was a pilot in the U.S. Air Force and became an astronaut in 1963. In 1966, he orbited Earth aboard the *Gemini 12* spacecraft, where he performed both docking operations with another space vehicle and extravehicular activities (EVAs). Because of his expertise in this area, he was chosen as a member of the Apollo crew and became the second human to set foot on the Moon. He retired from the air force in 1972 and wrote two books about his activities in the space program, *Return to Earth* and *Men from Earth*.

Neil Armstrong (1930–2012)

Armstrong was a U.S. Navy pilot, and joined the National Advisory Committee for Aeronautics (NACA) in 1952, which was later replaced by the National Aeronautics and Space Administration (NASA). He became an astronaut in 1962 and flew his first space mission as commander of *Gemini 8* in 1966. As commander of *Apollo 11*, he became the first person to step on the Moon. He briefly served as deputy associate administrator for aeronautics at NASA headquarters, where he was responsible for the coordination and management of research and technology. He left NASA in 1971 to teach and to act as spokesperson for several different businesses.

Michael Collins (b. 1930)

Collins was a fighter pilot and experimental test pilot in the U.S. Air Force. In 1963, he became a NASA astronaut and piloted the three-day *Gemini 10* mission in 1966. His second flight was as Command Module pilot aboard *Apollo 11*. He remained in the Moon's orbit while Armstrong and Aldrin landed and walked on the lunar surface. After retiring from NASA in 1970, he briefly held a position in the U.S. Department of State as assistant secretary of state for public affairs. The following year, he joined the Smithsonian Institution as the director of the National Air and Space Museum, where he was responsible for the construction of the new museum building in Washington, D.C.

Charles Moss Duke Jr. (b. 1935)

Duke was a brigadier general in the U.S. Air Force and a NASA astronaut. As lunar module pilot for *Apollo 16* in 1972, he became the tenth person to walk on the Moon. He served as capsule communicator (CAPCOM) on the *Apollo 11* launch, and was the voice of Mission Control in Houston, Texas, speaking to the astronauts during their historic voyage.

GLOSSARY

basalt hard, dense, dark rock formed by volcanic action

commemorate honor and remember an important event or person

contemplate think about something

contingency event that may occur but is not likely or intended; a possibility

crater large hole in the ground caused by something falling or exploding, such as a meteorite or a bomb

descent move from a higher to a lower place

desolation complete emptiness

Gemini second human U.S. spaceflight program whose goal was to develop space travel techniques for the Apollo program of landing a man on the Moon

Mercury first U.S. spaceflight program, which sent the first American into space

meteor piece of rock or metal in space that speeds into a heavenly body's atmosphere and forms a light as it burns and falls

National Aeronautics and Space Administration (NASA) U.S. government agency that is responsible for the space program

satellite spacecraft that is sent into orbit around Earth, the Moon, or another celestial body

ultraviolet invisible radiation wavelengths that can be harmful to living things

venture go somewhere or do something daring, dangerous, or unpleasant

FIND OUT MORE

Books

Dell, Pamela. *Man on the Moon: How a Photograph Made Anything Seem Possible*. Mankato, MN: Capstone, 2011.

Green, Carl R. *Walking on the Moon: The Amazing* Apollo 11 *Mission*. Berkeley Heights, NJ: Enslow, 2012.

Morris, Neil. *What Does Space Exploration Do for Us? (Earth, Space, and Beyond)*. Chicago: Raintree, 2012.

Oxlade, Chris. *The Moon (Astronaut Travel Guides)*. Chicago: Heinemann, 2013.

Snedden, Robert. *Exploring Space (Sci-Hi)*. Chicago: Raintree, 2010.

DVDs

First Moonwalk: The Restored Apollo 11 *EVA*. Spacecraft Films, 2010.

Footprints on the Moon: Apollo 11 *1969*. VCI Entertainment, 2010.

Journey to the Moon: The 40th Anniversary of Apollo 11. Mill Creek Entertainment, 2009.

Moon Landing: The Apollo 11. Biografilm, 2008.

Web Sites

news.nationalgeographic.com/news/2009/07/090715-moon
-landing-apollo-facts.html
This site offers facts and figures on *Apollo 11*'s historic flight.

science.howstuffworks.com/lunar-landing.htm
This site offers text and photos that explain the *Apollo 11* mission, the Space Race, and other Apollo moon landings.

science.nasa.gov/science-news/science-at-nasa/2006/19jul
_seaoftranquillity/
This site features the official NASA retelling of the moon landing and links to photo galleries.